THE GOOD EARTH

NOTES

including
- *Life and Background*
- *Introduction*
- *List of Characters*
- *Critical Commentaries*
- *Character Analyses*
- *The Chinese Custom of Foot-Binding*
- *Lotus Flower and Concubinage*
- *Review Questions*
- *Selected Bibliography*
- The Good Earth *Genealogy*

by
Stephen Veo Huntley, M.A.
University of Nebraska

Cliffs Notes

INCORPORATED

LINCOLN, NEBRASKA 68501

Editor	Consulting Editor
Gary Carey, M.A.	*James L. Roberts, Ph.D.*
University of Colorado	*Department of English*
	University of Nebraska

ISBN 0-8220-0535-2
© Copyright 1974, 1990
by
Cliffs Notes, Inc.
All Rights Reserved
Printed in U.S.A.

1996 Printing

The Cliffs Notes logo, the names "Cliffs" and "Cliffs Notes," and the black and yellow diagonal-stripe cover design are all registered trademarks belonging to Cliffs Notes, Inc., and may not be used in whole or in part without written permission.

Cliffs Notes, Inc.   Lincoln, Nebraska

CONTENTS

The Good Earth Notes

LIFE AND BACKGROUND

With our official recognition of the People's Republic of China and its emergence as a world power, it is evident now that our future is in many ways linked to that of the Chinese people. Awareness of the Chinese is reflected in a noticeable upswing of interest in Chinese culture, philosophy, and religion. Pearl S. Buck was truly a pioneer in this appreciation and, through her writings and humanitarian activities, she often made attempts to reduce the cultures of China and the United States to their lowest common denominator in order to bridge the two worlds in which she lived.

Although Pearl Sydenstricker was born in America (1892), she was taken to China by her missionary parents when she was only a few months old. She spoke Chinese before she spoke English, played with Chinese children, and listened intently to the Buddhist and Taoist legends related to her by her Chinese nurse. She later called these legends her first literary influence. Another strong influence on the young girl was her mother, Caroline Sydenstricker, who told stories about America to Pearl. She also read books available to her: *Tom Sawyer, Huckleberry Finn,* and various works of Shakespeare, Scott, Thackeray, George Eliot and, especially, Dickens.

Her love of these stories and her interest in people's lives made Pearl Buck determined at an early age to become a writer of stories. As she later writes in *My Several Worlds:* "Even then I had intended to be a teller of tales, a writer of novels, though how that end was to be achieved I did not know. One longs to make what one loves, and above all I loved to hear stories about people. I was a nuisance of a child, I fear, always curious to know about people and why they were as I found them." Aided by her mother's encouragement, Pearl got her first youthful selections published in the children's section of the *Shanghai Mercury.*

Because of her childhood in China, Pearl Buck was very sympathetic with many aspects of Chinese culture. At an early age, she studied Confucian scholarship and Chinese history. Later, she worked in an institution to rehabilitate slave girls who had fled from the cruel treatment of their owners. These experiences made Pearl aware not only of the evils and injustices within the Chinese culture, but also made her sympathetic to the plight of the Chinese at the hands of Western imperialism. She personally felt the results of this exploitation in 1905 when her family, though each member had been a dear friend to the Chinese of the village, was forced to flee to the seacoast for protection during the Boxer Rebellion. For the first time, Pearl realized that she was somehow an alien, only a visitor in the only world of which she had any direct experience.

At the age of seventeen (1909), Pearl Sydenstricker came to the United States to attend Randolph-Macon Woman's College. Here she continued to write stories and even co-authored a class play. In her senior year, her writing talent won two literary prizes. Her experience in the United States soon made her aware that her life and education in China were far different from that of girls in the United States. Once again, she had to accept the fact that she was different, and she made efforts to bridge her two worlds.

After receiving her degree in 1914, she remained at Randolph-Macon as a teaching assistant in the department of Philosophy and Psychology. This position was short-lived, however, for Pearl was soon called back to China when her mother became seriously ill at the end of 1914. While caring for her mother, Pearl studied written Chinese and took her mother's place as a counselor, listening to Chinese women's viewpoints and helping them solve their problems.

On May 13, 1917, Pearl married John Lossing Buck, an American agricultural expert. John, originally from upstate New

York, was in China with the Presbyterian Mission Board, teaching American farming methods to the Chinese. The Bucks lived in the city of Nanhsüchou in the Anhwei province of North China. It is here that Pearl Buck became acquainted with the life of the Chinese peasant—his simple life and farming methods, his precarious fights against drought, famine, death, and his close ties with the earth. This knowledge and love of the Chinese peasant were to appear later in *The Good Earth* and other of her literary works.

In 1921, the Bucks moved south to Nanking, where John received a position at the University of Nanking as a professor of agricultural methods. Pearl also obtained a position as a teacher of English literature. In October of that year, Pearl's mother died, inspiring Pearl Buck to write a short biography of Mrs. Sydenstricker as a memorial to her family. This biography, Pearl's first book, was put away for many years, later revised, and was finally published as *The Exile* in 1936.

Mrs. Buck's life in Nanking was markedly different from the simple life in North China. Here, Western ideas were replacing traditional Chinese customs, and Bolshevist ideas were threatening the traditional Chinese political and social structures. The Chinese youth of Nanking were both seduced and confused by these rapidly changing ideas. Pearl Buck, through her work at the University of Nanking, was very aware of this confusion and rebellion and used them in Chapters 12, 13, and 14 of *The Good Earth*. During these years she also wrote many essays on the changes within China, some of which appeared in *The Atlantic Monthly, Forum,* and *The Nation.*

In 1925, John and Pearl Buck brought their first child to the United States, hoping that medical treatment could correct what they feared were signs of mental disorder. Unfortunately, they found that the girl would always be mentally retarded. While in the United States, Pearl and John both attended Cornell University where, in the following year, Pearl took her Master of Arts degree in English literature. To help finance this trip to the United States, Pearl entered and won the Laura Messenger Prize in history for her essay "China and the West," again bringing together her two worlds.

In late 1926, Pearl and John Buck returned to their Nanking home to teach at Southeastern University and the University of Nanking, respectively. However, in March of 1927, Nationalist soldiers attacked Nanking and began killing Caucasians. Pearl, John, their daughter, and Pearl's father were forced to flee Nanking for Shanghai, just as her family had fled during the Boxer Rebellion in 1905. Among the possessions which she was forced to leave behind was a completed but unpublished novel which was destroyed by the looting soldiers. Fortunately, the biography of her mother was left untouched, as was an incomplete novel, which, in 1930, became *East Wind: West Wind*, her first published novel.

In 1931, Pearl Buck published *The Good Earth*, the novel which won the 1932 Pulitzer Prize and international recognition. In the years from 1931-35, she published several other works, including *Sons* (1932) and *A House Divided* (1935), which were published with *The Good Earth* as a trilogy in 1935. This trilogy, *House of Earth*, was awarded the William Dean Howells Medal by the American Academy of Arts and Letters as the finest work of fiction within the years 1930-35.

Also in 1935, Pearl was divorced from John Lossing Buck and, on June 11, she married Richard J. Walsh, president of John Day Publishing Company. For the rest of her career, however, she continued writing under the name of Pearl S. Buck.

In 1936, Pearl Buck published two biographies which, with *The Good Earth*, would play a dominant role in her winning the Nobel Prize for Literature in 1938. The first of these was *The Exile*, a frank portrayal of Miss Buck's mother as an American girl and her missionary life in China. The second was *Fighting Angel*, a biography of Pearl's father, developed from a biographical sketch entitled "In Memoriam: Absalom Sydenstricker, 1852-1931," written shortly after his death. These two biographies were published together in 1944 as *The Spirit and the Flesh*.

After winning the Nobel Prize, Pearl Buck continued her writing with the same tremendous industry and extended her repertoire to include many genres. Her non-fiction works include *Tell the People* (1945), dealing with mass education; *The Child Who Never Grew* (1950), dealing with her retarded daughter; an autobiography, *My Several Worlds* (1954); *The Kennedy Women* (1970), telling of the strength and suffering of the women surrounding the Kennedys; and *Pearl Buck's Oriental Cookbook* (1972). Besides writing later Oriental novels, such as *Pavilion of Women* (1946), she also wrote such American works as *American Triptych* (1958), containing three novels first published under the pen name John Sedges: *The Townsman*, *Voices in the House*, and *The Long Love*.

Also contained within her vast writings are such plays as *Flight into China* (1939), *The First Wife* (1945), and *A Desert Incident* (1959). She wrote a novel treating the suppression of women, *This Proud Heart* (1938). Reaching into other media, she co-authored a musical production, *Christine* (1960), wrote radio scripts during World War II, and the movie script for *Satan Never Sleeps* (1962), from an outline by Leo McCarey.

Always a humanitarian who felt the results of racial prejudice while in China during the Boxer Rebellion in 1905 and the uprisings of 1927, Pearl Buck took up such causes as the suffering immigrants of New York City in the *New York Times* (November 16, 1954); India's fight for independence (she was one of the Mahatma Gandhi Memorial Foundation founders), and the Training School at Vineland, New Jersey, for the caring and treatment of the mentally retarded. Miss Buck also served as a member of the national committee of the American Civil Liberties Union and often spoke out for intellectual freedom and against censorship.

But perhaps Miss Buck's greatest interest was in children. She was the author of a great many children's books, as well as articles on unwanted children and adoption. In 1949, she and her husband, Richard Walsh, founded Welcome Home, an adoption agency for children of Asian-American blood, especially children of servicemen who had served overseas.

In all, she was the author of over sixty books, touching sympathetically on many subjects. Especially after winning the Nobel Prize in 1938, her humanitarian preoccupations often suppressed the objective frankness of her earlier works. There are, however, moments of greatness in all of her works and surely *The Good Earth* and the Nobel Prize biographies will stand as classics of literature for their simplicity of style and character portrayal.

INTRODUCTION

To better understand *The Good Earth,* a brief review of the history of China at that time would be helpful. After the overthrow of the Ching Dynasty of the Manchus in 1911 by Sun Yatsen and other dedicated intellectuals who envisioned a united and democratic nation, developments did not go quite as well as the leaders had hoped.

Since China is one of the largest nations on earth, it is natural that its people are not necessarily homogeneous. Even though they are basically of the same race and write the same language, there are at least a hundred spoken dialects. This means that a man from one province may not easily understand what a man from another province is saying; in many cases, verbal communication is totally impossible. However, an educated man could read Chinese, be it written by a man from the extreme South or a man from the extreme North, even though these two men would not understand each other's speech. As Wang Lung notes in Chapter 12: "But Anhwei is not Kiangsu. In Anhwei, where Wang Lung was born, the language is slow and deep and it wells from the throat. But in the Kiangsu city where they now lived the people spoke in syllables which splintered from their lips and from the ends of their tongues."

While perhaps over-simplifying the troubles in China after the overthrow of the Imperial power, most of the local military governors of the provinces were unwilling to be lorded over by what they considered a revolutionary government. Instead, they set up their own separate territories. This state of affairs went on for years.

Almost every province had its "strong man." They were popularly known as "war lords." Some were merely terrorists or bandits, but others controlled vast areas and held millions in thrall. Wu Pei-fu, for example, ruled five provinces in North and Central China and his "subjects" must have been well over one hundred million. In Manchuria, Chang Tso-ling held onto a territory almost as large as France and Spain combined. Even after his death at the hands of Japanese extremists, his son, the "Young Marshal," ruled until the Japanese finally took over in 1932 and established the satellite state of Manchukuo. The war lords collected taxes and had their own armies and civil service: their word was law. Even Chiang Kai-shek, while he pursued his goal of a united China, could have been labeled a war lord. After the death of Sun Yet-sen in 1925, and a period of struggle within the ruling Kuomintang party, Chiang finally set up his head-quarters in Nanking and his campaign against the local chieftains was largely successful until it became a conflict against the Communists of Mao Tse-tung and the Japanese.

By the late 1920s, the period which most resembles the period of this book, China was torn by civil strife from Canton to Peking, from the India border to the Amur River on the border of Russia. The lot of the Chinese peasant was not very good. Most of them were tenant farmers, working the land for the rich landowners, who may have owned thousands of acres (as does Wang Lung at the end of *The Good Earth*). But here and there were small, independent farmers working their own plots, as does Wang Lung at the beginning of the novel. These small farmers were constantly at the prey of marauding bandits – such as Wang Lung's uncle and the "red beards." They were also at the mercy of the grain merchants since they could not read or write; hence, the importance for Wang Lung to have his oldest son learn to read and write. Essentially, however, most of the farmers were left alone, for even the war lords had to eat. The farmer was thus protected to some extent by the same needs which plagued him and his family.

In times of favorable weather, the peasant lived a frugal but adequate life. He saw very little of actual money (during the first part of the novel, a piece of silver was a very rare thing for Wang Lung), but he usually had enough to eat, though it might be no more than garlic and unleavened bread. Wang Lung was often scorned by those who had education or an ability for commerce, and people often called him "Wang, the farmer" in a derogatory manner and held their nose in contempt for the garlic he ate. But in spite of these things, the small landowning peasant had a pride in the land he owned, and this pride is Wang Lung's most distinguishing characteristic. His final speech in the novel concerns the importance of retaining his land and never selling even a small portion of it.

Some critics have claimed that Pearl Buck is not writing about a Chinese farmer, but a universal farmer, one who knows that his riches and his security come from the good earth itself. This concept does give a universality to the novel, but for most readers the importance of the novel lies in Pearl Buck's knowledge of China and of the Chinese – a knowledge as great as that which any foreigner can possess. Her life in the rural areas of China also gave her a profound insight into the thinking of the Chinese peasant, something that Mao Tse-tung discovered when he was planning his revolution, and the Communist leader eventually came to depend on farmers like Wang Lung, with their strength of character, as a nucleus of his revolutionaries. Even Wang Lung's third son, we hear, became an important official in the revolutionary army.

LIST OF CHARACTERS

In Chinese names, the last name is always written first. Thus, at the end of the novel, we discover that we have the House of Wang, not the House of Lung. Also in China, it was a rather common habit to refer to a person by his profession or rank. Wang was often referred to as "Wang, the farmer," as when he was greeted by Cuckoo upon his initial visit to the tea house.

And, finally, many characters are not named but are designated by their relationship to one another, such as Wang Lung's uncle's son.

Wang Lung

The Chinese farmer who rises from a peasant farmer, struggling for a living, to become the head of the powerful House of Wang.

O-lan

The wife whom he bought from the House of Hwang and who serves him diligently until her death.

Wang Lung's Father

An elderly man at the beginning of the book who serves mainly to show how the elderly are respected and treated.

Wang Lung's Uncle

A lazy and vicious man whom Wang Lung resents but, according to custom, he must take him into his house because he is a paternal relative.

The Uncle's Wife

A fat and overbearing gossip who has no control over her children. She makes the arrangements for Lotus Flower to become Wang Lung's concubine.

The Uncle's Son

He introduces Wang Lung's eldest son to prostitutes and later tries to seduce Wang Lung's daughter.

Eldest Son (Nun En)

Wang Lung takes him from the fields and educates him; ironically, the son later feels contempt for the land.

Second Son (Nun Wen)

He is also given an education but he uses his knowledge in order to increase the wealth of the House of Wang.

Third Son

An unusually quiet boy who also demands an education; he later joins one of the revolutionary armies.

Eldest Daughter ("poor fool")

Wang Lung often refers to his eldest daughter as his "poor fool" because she was born just prior to the famine and, as a result, never developed mentally.

Youngest Daughter

Wang Lung's prettiest daughter whom he must place in the house of her betrothed in order to keep the uncle's son from her.

Lotus Flower

A prostitute in a tea house who captivates Wang Lung; he later purchases her as his concubine.

Cuckoo

Originally, she lived with the Old Lord in the House of Hwang; later, she came to the House of Wang as a servant to Lotus.

Pear Blossom

A young slave bought during a famine. She prefers the quiet ardors of old men to the fiery passions of young men.

Ching

Wang Lung's neighbor who sells his land and becomes the trusted overseer of Wang Lung's lands.

Liu

The grain merchant whom the second son works for and who will provide a wife for the eldest Wang son. He also accepts Wang Lung's youngest daughter for his son's wife.

Yang

An ugly prostitute who is visited by Wang Lung's eldest son.

The Old Lord Hwang and the Old Mistress Hwang

Through his concubines and her addiction to opium, these two people represent the decadence of the rich.

CRITICAL COMMENTARIES

CHAPTERS 1-2

In these first two chapters, we are immediately introduced to the main theme of the novel—man's basic relationship with the earth and how he gains strength and sustenance from it. Wang Lung, the central character of the novel, feels a deep respect for the earth. We discover that his house is made of earth and even his gods before whom he places incense are also made of earth. Thus he gains his food, his shelter, and his religion from the earth. As Pearl Buck notes, everything comes out of the earth, but ultimately everything returns to the earth.

Wang Lung's relationship with the earth is not an intellectual one; instead, it is simple and basic. Wang Lung has "no articulate thought on anything; there was only this perfect sympathy of movement, of turning this earth of theirs over and over to the sun, this earth which formed their home and fed their bodies and made their gods."

Another theme that is introduced is the contrast between the simplicity and innocence of Wang Lung and the luxury, opulence, and decadence of the House of Hwang. For Wang Lung, it is a luxury even to have a bath before he goes for his bride, and he has to measure out each ounce of food so as to have enough to invite a few humble guests into his house. In contrast, when he arrives in town, he is made fun of by the barbers, and he feels uncomfortable and embarrassed at the House of Hwang.

He is taken advantage of by the gateman because of his rough appearance and his lack of knowledge. The reader should keep this scene in mind when Wang Lung later returns with his first-born child and is dressed in a new coat of black cloth. Then he is treated with more respect. Ultimately, one should remember that Wang Lung will become the owner of this house where he once trembled as a rough, uncouth peasant.

These first two chapters immediately establish the social concept that a woman is an inferior person to a man. At this time, women were bought and sold as slaves, and Wang Lung does buy O-lan from the House of Hwang. The woman has to walk six paces behind the man, and she does not speak unless spoken to. Furthermore, Wang Lung's father pretends not even to notice her when they arrive home for the first time. Wang Lung is pleased that he will no longer have to do certain chores to manage his household. This sense of superiority extends to Wang Lung's being embarrassed because he does not know whether or not he satisfied O-lan. "He was ashamed of his own curiosity and of his interest in her. She was, after all, only a woman."

Initially, Wang Lung's greatest disappointment with O-lan is that her feet were not bound. In the Chinese culture, small feet (achieved through painful binding: see the section on foot-binding) were considered a mark of elegance and beauty. Women who had their feet bound could not walk long distances nor even stand for longer than a few minutes. Thus, if O-lan's feet had been bound, she would never have been able to work in the fields and help Wang Lung become a prosperous farmer. It is ironic that, because of O-lan's hard work, Wang Lung can later afford to buy Lotus Flower as his concubine, and we should remember that Lotus Flower has to be carried to Wang Lung's house because her bound feet are too delicate to make the journey.

When Wang Lung and O-lan burn incense before the god and goddess of earth, we witness, as it were, their marriage ceremony. The rings and earrings accepted earlier are part of the ritual, but the marriage is only real when it is consummated that night. O-lan cannot even appear before the male guests until she has become his wife in the most physical sense.

Perhaps one of the greatest values of this novel is its attempt to present for the Western reader a clear view of the Chinese culture — a culture that is vastly different from Western civilization. Pearl Buck captures this culture with complete objectivity. Her style is simple and straightforward, and her presentation of characters is also simple and straightforward. We thus have the impression that we are receiving an accurate, journalistic account of the life of a representative Chinese farmer.

CHAPTERS 3-6

At the end of Chapter 2, O-lan announced that she was "with child." Beginning with Chapter 3, Wang Lung immediately begins to assume that the child will be a "man child." As we are soon to learn, a girl child was considered a burden, if not a disgrace, whereas a man child was a benefit to the family. This concept develops mainly out of Chinese customs and their religion of ancestor worship. If a man has sons, he never has to worry — his sons will take care of him. Furthermore, this belief is so strong that a son has virtually no rights of his own as long as his father is alive. Even Wang Lung's uncle can bully or hit Wang Lung and, according to religion and custom, Wang Lung can do nothing but accept this relationship status. We know that he secretly resents his uncle, but, publicly, he cannot oppose him.

O-lan's character is further developed in these chapters. Previously, we saw her working side by side with Wang Lung while, at the same time, taking care of the house and cooking. Now we see that she works in the fields until she comes into labor. We see that she is a very proud woman because she refuses to have anyone from the House of Hwang help her during childbirth. Wang Lung tells her that even his own mother had help during childbirth, but she stubbornly refuses to have anyone help her. The only help she requests is a newly peeled and slit reed to "cut the child's life from mine." Even in the midst of labor, she takes time to prepare food for Wang Lung and his father. It is now that Wang Lung discovers that "she was a woman such as is not commonly found." She then retires to the room to give birth to her baby, and even cleans up after giving birth before she calls Wang Lung to come and see his man child. Early in the novel, then, Pearl Buck establishes O-lan as an exceptional person, one who is proud, independent, stubborn, and resourceful.

With the help of O-lan, their resourcefulness and frugality begin to pay off. Unlike most other women, O-lan makes their own shoes, she repairs all of the broken pots, and she mends the clothing while Wang Lung is repairing the tools and mending the farm equipment. In terms of food, O-lan is an expert at making a little bit go a long way. Wang Lung is pleased that he does not have to spend money on fuel because O-lan collects wood, and the land is improved because she collects the droppings of horses and donkeys in the road.

By the end of Chapter 4, Wang Lung has saved enough money that he can now "walk with his fellows . . . at ease with himself and with all." The change is seen even further when he returns in Chapter 6 to the House of Hwang. He is now dressed in a new black cloth suit, which O-lan has made, in addition to the clothing for the newborn child. When Wang Lung reaches the door of the House of Hwang, his inner assurance creates new respect from the gateman. As a contrast to the time when he first came and the gateman made fun of him, he is now seated in the gateman's house and is presented tea, which he scorns "as though it were not good enough in quality" for him.

This new assurance is also seen when he refers to Hwang's land as though he were an equal to Hwang or as though he were referring to Ching's land—Ching being the neighboring farmer who will later become Wang Lung's overseer. And, finally, at the end of Chapter 6, Wang Lung is able to buy a piece of land that belongs to the House of Hwang. This is the beginning of the descent of the House of Hwang and the rise of the House of Wang.

It is important to note in this chapter that, for the Chinese, the color "red" carried special significance and was used in all types of ceremonies. Wang Lung gets some red dye to color the eggs in celebration of the birth of his first son. O-lan wants to dress her son in red silk before carrying him before the Old Mistress. In weddings of affluence, the bride is always dressed in red. In Chapter 5, to celebrate the new year, red paper is used to make good luck signs and to make new clothes for the gods. Red signs are put on the doorway and on various items of furniture, and the people burn two red candles on the event of the new year.

As a simple peasant, Wang Lung has no consistent religious pattern in his life. Instead, he uses various aspects of several religions. Mainly, however, he is concerned with superstitions and evil omens. When he thinks in Chapter 5 that he is too lucky to have such a child, he begins to refer to the child as an ugly girl because the evil spirits will not be interested in a mere girl. These fears come to Wang Lung as a result of the rumors that the House of Hwang is in trouble. He therefore wants to ward off any evil spirits which might affect his rise.

By the end of Chapter 6, O-lan has given birth to a second son, and Wang Lung does not feel the need this time to celebrate because he now realizes that O-lan has brought him exceptional good fortune and that there will be sons every year. Note here, too, that the harvest is better than ever and the piece of rice land that he bought from the House of Hwang yielded much more than his own land.

CHAPTERS 7-9

In this section Wang Lung and his family are plagued with bad luck which overshadows even the good fortune of the preceding section. In Chapter 7, Wang Lung's uncle begins to be the "trouble which Wang Lung had surmised from the beginning that he might be." Throughout this section, the uncle takes advantage of the claims of relationship which he holds over Wang Lung by asking him for a dowry for his daughter in Chapter 7 and for food during the drought in Chapter 8.

To justify these demands, the uncle calls himself a "man of evil destiny." Here, he brings this evil to Wang Lung's house. By the end of Chapter 7, Wang Lung is struck with a sense of evil as his third child is born a daughter, one who does not belong to her parents, but is "born and reared for other families." Chapter 7 is concluded by the "evil omen" of a flock of crows.

Drought in Chapter 8 plagues the whole village. Again the uncle brings trouble to the family of Wang Lung with claims of "filial impiety" and rumors that Wang Lung is hoarding food. O-lan is again with child, a child which Wang Lung especially dreads as the famine intensifies. It is declared fortunate that it dies soon after birth. Now we see an angry Wang Lung, cursing the Old Man in Heaven, spitting on the gods at the temple of earth, but defiantly hanging onto life for himself and his family.

After the first year's drought, Wang Lung sells his meager harvest immediately, instead of saving it to sell when the prices go up during the winter. With the profit, he buys another piece of land and does not tell even O-lan about it. This time, when he goes to see the agent for the House of Hwang, Wang Lung is placed on a position closer to equality, because the House of Hwang is in desperate need of money. Consequently, the "evil times" have made the two families more equal.

The land—the earth—remains for Wang Lung the most important thing of his life. Even though his family is starving, he still feels the importance of the land. He knows that if he had silver that the townspeople would have stolen it from him but "they cannot take the land from me." And when his uncle comes with some opportunists, Wang Lung still refuses to sell his land: "I shall never sell the land. . . . Bit by bit I will dig up the fields and feed the earth itself to the children and when they die I will bury them in the land, and I and my wife and my old father, even he, will die on the land that has given us birth." Then, by selling their household effects, they get a meager two pieces of silver and begin their journey to the south.

Wang Lung's uncle and Ching, the neighboring farmer, are further developed in this chapter. The uncle is the most vicious and evil person in the novel. Wang Lung was earlier embarrassed that the uncle allowed his fifteen-year-old daughter to walk the streets talking to men. He is also ashamed that his uncle carries the same name as he does. The uncle is the person responsible for the townspeople pillaging Wang Lung's house and, even after causing the pillaging, he still brings some opportunists to see Wang Lung. In addition, the uncle still uses his family ties to demand money from Wang Lung.

In contrast, Ching feels guilty about his role in the pillaging and we hear that he would not have participated if extreme hunger had not forced him to do so. Ching atones for his participation by giving a few beans to Wang Lung. This act will later make Ching a trusted and favored person in Wang Lung's eyes, whereas Wang Lung will forever resent everything about his uncle.

The young girl child, whom Wang Lung calls his "little fool" in this chapter, will actually become his fool because, due to the famine, she will become a retarded child. However, throughout the rest of the novel, Wang Lung will take pleasure in being with his "fool."

The lowest point in Wang Lung's life is reached in this chapter when he has to bury his own child. He is so weak himself that when he notices the two bruised spots on the child's neck, obviously made when O-lan put the pathetic child out of her existence, he cannot even make a judgment about the situation. When he has not the strength to bury the child and has to leave it, he knows that the starving dog will eat it immediately. He is, "for the first time, wholly filled with despair."

CHAPTERS 10-11

The first sentence of Chapter 10 emphasizes the relationship between Wang Lung and the land. He can leave his house in order to go south and do no more than "pull the door right upon its wooden hinges and fasten the iron hasp." And in Chapter 15, when he returns, he takes up the land as he left it. This emphasizes the continuation of the land with the owner. Wang Lung and his family have been gone for a few years, and yet when they return, the land is still intact and is still theirs.

Note here that Wang Lung's religion fluctuates with his personal fortunes. Earlier, when he was fortunate, he gave incense to the little earth gods. Now that he is forced to leave his land, he walks right by the "little temple with the two small stately gods within, who never notice anything that passed." Wang Lung's religion is not a coherent set of beliefs—instead, it is the combination of many types of superstitions that are common to a primitve person.

Wang Lung passes the House of Hwang and he is bitter about the fortunes of the rich. Later on, we must remember that he gets rich because he and O-lan participate in the pillaging of a house of a rich lord in the "southern city" and that still further on, when Wang Lung's wealth is established, he is also invaded by an army of revolutionaries. The "thousand curses to the parents that bore the children of Hwang" will ultimately become a type of curse on the House of Wang, particularly as Wang's children begin to revolt against their father.

Wang Lung's provincialism is also emphasized in this chapter as he acknowledges that he has heard of "firewagons" (trains), but he has never seen one, much less ridden on one. Again, as in the title, Pearl Buck is emphasizing the relationship of the farmer with his good earth. As Wang Lung says in this chapter, it is not "well for a man to know more than is necessary for his daily living." The main concern of this first part of the novel is the matter of ekeing out the necessities for everyday living.

As they leave their home and village, we are made aware that the little girl child is in dire circumstances. The starvation which accompanies her early years will have a disastrous effect on her. The fact that Wang Lung has to hold her so close to his breast prevents him from selling her as a "slave" later on when the family gets into critical straits. And it is also this starvation which later leads to her being retarded, yet Wang Lung will always take pleasure in her presence, even after he has gained great wealth.

With Chapter 11, the reader feels the intense relief that, for the first time in days, the family is able to buy a little rice for sustenance. Also, they learn how to make a shelter out of six mats, and ultimately how to survive in the new land. They also learn how a man can beg for a living. This entire concept is alien to Wang Lung, who has owned his *own land*. The stranger laughs, saying that a man can make more money begging than working in the south. So it is, at the end of the chapter, for much money has been made by begging as was made by the totally exhausting work which left Wang Lung's hands ripped to shreds and his body enervated. But as one who owns land in another part of the country, he retains those values which are associated with the land and he will not resort to begging.

The strength of O-lan serves the family well here since she is able to remember when her own family was in a situation similar to the one they are now in. For the first time, we hear that O-lan was once in a position as desperate as they are now in. She knows how to build their house from the mats, and she teaches the family how to beg. When the children don't realize the desperate circumstances, she slaps them until they are "fit to beg." We are constantly surprised at the amount of resources that O-lan has. Once more, Wang Lung is surprised at her: "How much there was of this woman he did not know!"

Many things surprise Wang Lung about the city, but most of all he is surprised at the plentitude. Unlike his homeland, where no amount of money could buy food simply because it did not exist, here there are well-fed people, meat and vegetables in the markets, and fresh fish swimming in tubs of water. Surely no man could starve in this land of plenty. They have so much food, as the man on the "firewagon" said early in Chapter 11, that for a penny one can have as much white rice gruel as his belly can hold.

Perhaps more surprising for Wang Lung is the fact that there are people that give to the poor. Surely, Wang Lung feels, these must be the best of men; surely they "must do it out of a good heart." But the guard better expresses the true motives of the gentry when he says that they do it "for a good deed for the future" or that they "may get merit in heaven" or "for righteousness that men may speak well of them." This guard's cynicism and bitterness toward the gentry sets the tone for the undercurrents of revolution in the following chapters.

The importance of family ties is again emphasized in this section when Wang Lung's father refuses to beg for food. The father points out that he has done his duty by siring a "son and son's sons"; thus it would be an insult to family ties to expect him to beg.

CHAPTERS 12-14

Chapter 12 presents the difficulties which Wang Lung and his family have in adjusting to the new and different ways in this southern city. Among the difficulties is a language barrier. This city speaks in a dialect which makes it extremely difficult for Wang Lung to understand it. He feels alien here and will constantly long to return to his land.

Wang Lung gradually learns things about the city and becomes more adept with his ricksha but is still unable to earn money enough to begin saving. Everything must go for the necessity of food. Throughout these chapters, a contrast is shown between the very poor living among plentitude, but not being able to share in it. The underlying feelings of discontent and revolution in the city begin to come to the forefront in this section and are finally climaxed by the looting of the rich man's house. The contrast between the gentry and the poor people of the city is emphasized by the contrast drawn between Wang Lung and the rich man. "He lived in the rich city as alien as a rat in a rich man's house that is fed on scraps thrown away."

When Wang Lung discovers that his children, especially the second son, have resorted to stealing, Wang Lung's desire to return to his land is intensified. He cannot tolerate the idea of a man who owns land having a son who has to steal. He does not eat of the meat that the second son steals and even considers selling his daughter. The irony is that while he beats his second son for stealing a piece of meat, he takes gold from the fat old man and is later delighted with the jewels which O-lan was able to steal from the secret hiding place in the rich man's house.

As Wang Lung sees men being forced into service by soldiers, he gives up his job with the ricksha and accepts a night job which pays even less. Thus, his situation is gradually worsening and he still thinks of selling his "fool" so that the family can return to the land. O-lan tells him to wait because there is unrest in the city and she is anticipating that something favorable will happen.

In addition to the episodes with the soldiers, there are other explicit examples of unrest in the city. There is the young man who speaks of revolution; he condemns the rich and would divide the wealth of the rich among the poor. Also, there is the old man from the family in an adjoining hut who maintains that "when the rich are too rich, there is a way, and if I am not mistaken that way will come soon." Finally, there is an uprising when the gates of the rich are broken and the poor pour into the houses to pillage. Thus, it is by the opportunism of Wang Lung that he is able to get enough money to return to the land just at the point when he had decided that he must sell his "fool," even against his most basic principles.

Chapter 14 ends Wang Lung's first separation from the land. The chapter ends with his triumphant cry: "We go back to the land—tomorrow we go back to the land!"

CHAPTERS 15-17

With the money which Wang Lung opportunistically received, he immediately makes plans to return to his "good earth" as soon as possible. He buys good seed from the south, even seeds which he has never planted before—such seeds as celery, lotus, and "fragrant red beans." He is so pleased to be returning to his good earth that he pays more for an ox than he should have paid. But his sense of being once again close to his land allows him this extravagance.

When he returns home, he finds that the peach trees and other trees are budding and the land is ready for planting. He receives strength from the land and, "for a long time it seemed to Wang Lung that he wished to see no human being but only to be alone on his land." Again, Pearl Buck emphasizes the importance of the land and how Wang Lung takes his strength from the land.

When Wang Lung's neighbor, Ching, visits him, Wang Lung volunteers to help Ching plow his land. Unlike Wang Lung, who refused as long as possible to sell his "fool," we discover that Ching was forced to give his own daughter away in order to keep her from dying of starvation. Wang Lung has never forgotten that Ching gave O-lan a few beans to chew on so as to get through her labor before they left for the south. At this time also, we discover that rumors associate Wang Lung's uncle with bandits; Wang Lung, however, is only thankful that his uncle is not here. The fact that the uncle is connected with the marauding bandits will later carry greater significance during the winter of the flood — when Wang Lung would have been raided by bandits if his uncle were not a part of the group.

As always, Wang Lung's view of the gods follows the rise and fall of his own fortunes. Now that his fortune is on the rise, he again takes notice of the condition of his gods. He passes them and sees that the rains have washed away their clay faces and that their clothes are in tatters. He mildly reproaches them for their condition, reminding them that this is what happens "to gods who do evil to men!" But at the end of Chapter 15, he takes some incense to the gods because "they have power over earth."

In Chapter 15, we again see the resourceful qualities of O-lan as she repairs tools, the house, and anything else that needs to be done. Also, we discover that she was astute enough to know where the people in great houses keep their riches and she was able to grab a large amount of jewels. Once again, Wang Lung is "filled with admiration" for this woman whom he has married. Now Wang Lung wants to use the jewels to buy more land. He feels great security with land because no one can take the land away from a person — "for nothing else is safe" — except land.

We see another view of O-lan when she pleads to keep two pearls for herself. She has never had anything so delicate and so beautiful as these exquisite pearls. Wang Lung relents and allows her to keep the pearls, but in Chapters 18-19, when he becomes involved with Lotus, he takes them from her, a heartless action which he shall later regret.

Chapter 16 develops the idea that the fall of the House of Hwang is concomitant with the rise of the House of Wang in the next chapters. As Wang Lung approaches the impressive House of Hwang, he is shy, afraid, and reticent. He is still awed in the presence of such wealth. He is yet "half afraid, for all his life he half-feared the people in the great house." We hear also that the sons of old Hwang want him to sell as much of the land as is possible and to send them the money. They have sent word that they "cannot live in such a place. Let us sell and divide the money." Pearl Buck implies that the decline of the great House of Hwang is directly related to leaving and selling the land. A house is corrupted when the members are no longer close to the land. Therefore, Wang Lung resolves that his sons will always be close to the land. Ironically, at the end of the novel, his sons plan to sell the land as soon as they can, thus implying future corruption of the House of Wang.

In a sense, Wang Lung feels that there is something wrong with the demise of such an institution: "And the more he mused, the more monstrous it seemed that the great and rich family, who all his own life and all his father's and grandfather's lives long had been a power and a glory in the town, were now fallen and scattered." He concludes that "it comes of their leaving the land." Wang Lung's last comment in the novel, then, is this: there is extreme importance in remaining on the land.

In Chapter 17, having bought the Hwang land with the jewels, the rise of the House of Wang continues by Wang Lung asking Ching to sell him his land and to move in and be the over-seer of Wang Lung's land. Still feeling strongly about the impor-tance of the land, Wang Lung has his sons go with him to the fields, where he tries to teach them how to farm the land.

Since he is now wealthy, he does not allow O-lan to work in the fields with him. Soon, she gives birth to twins, a boy and a girl. And as the House of Wang increases in number, so does his wealth. He has taken care to build his fortunes so securely that when bad years come, he will have enough to carry him through and will never have to leave his lands. He has to hire more laborers every year and must build additions to his house.

As he becomes an important person, he realizes the need to have a son who can read and write because his own illiteracy has not only been a source of embarrassment to him, but it has also put him at the mercy of the grain merchants. Consequently, the first move away from the land occurs when Wang Lung sends his eldest son to school. The second son, upon hearing this, causes so much dissension that Wang Lung lets both of them go to school. And then, for the first time, the two sons are named: Nung En is the eldest and Nung Wen is the second son.

CHAPTERS 18-19

These chapters are marked by the coming of the flood waters after seven years of good harvests. During these seven years, Wang Lung's fortunes have increased and when, in the seventh year, a great flood covered most of his land, Wang Lung had stocked enough to not be adversely affected by the floods. He had food and money, and his house was on a hill far away from the water. Thus, his foresight has paid off and as others starved, Wang Lung had plenty.

With the coming of the waters, Wang Lung becomes bored with his house and its members. He cannot work in the fields, his father is growing feebleminded, his little "fool" only makes him sad, and O-lan's body no longer appeals to him. For the first time in his life, he begins to look critically at O-lan and to find fault with her. He realizes that she is a dull and common creature "who plodded in silence . . . her features were too large . . . and her feet were large and spreading."

We also learn that O-lan has "a fire in her vitals." Wang Lung is sincerely moved, but still cannot stem the irritation in his breast as he reproaches her for not oiling her hair, and again he is especially annoyed at her hideous "big feet."

Wang Lung leaves for town "without knowing what it was he wished." With increased trips to town, he begins to visit the tea house every day. After several visits, he meets Cuckoo in the tea house. Upon their encounter, she exclaims loudly: "Well, and Wang the farmer!" This encounter makes Wang Lung determined to show her that he is more than a "farmer." He is even half-ashamed that he has only had tea during all of these visits to the tea house and he is amazed when Cuckoo tells him that she can provide him with his choice of women, the "pictures of dream women, of goddesses in the mountain of Kwen Lwen." By the end of the chapter, what had earlier been a casual appreciation of the pictures turns to a process of selection of the girl whom Wang Lung finds most beautiful.

The series of incidents leading up to Wang Lung's courtship of Lotus Flower in Chapters 18-19 is presented by Pearl Buck as totally coincidental happenings. In Chapter 18, she tells us that his boredom with his family and home during the floods "might have been nothing if Wang Lung were still a poor man or if the water were not spread over his fields. But he had money." Later in the chapter, Pearl Buck tells us that he visited the tea house only for diversion and because of his boredom at home, and "so he might have continued for many days on end" had he not met Cuckoo at the tea house.

Chapter 19 begins with a similar statement of chance: "Now if the waters had at that time receded from Wang Lung's land . . . Wang Lung might never have gone again to the great tea shop. Or if a child had fallen ill or the old man had reached suddenly to the end of his days, Wang Lung might have been caught up in the new thing and so forgotten the painted face upon the scroll and the body and the woman slender as a bamboo." Even when Wang Lung had decided to go and meet this beautiful girl, he "hesitated upon the threshold and he stood in the bright light which streamed from the open doors. And he might have stood there and gone away," but out of the shadows came Cuckoo, who said, "Ah, it is only the farmer!"

It was, then, a series of coincidences and Wang Lung's injured pride that made him feel the need to show Cuckoo that he was lordly and rich enough to meet the woman. And it was the silver in his girdle that carried him past the insults of the other girls who disdained his garlicky smell. Throughout this section, Wang Lung is often ashamed of being a country bumpkin, much like his initial visit to town in Chapter 1.

When he is with Lotus Flower, Wang Lung admires her small hands, her long nails, and her delicate feet. All of these things

O-lan lacks, but the reader recalls that had O-lan possessed these things, she could not have helped Wang Lung in the fields during the lean years. Nevertheless, Lotus Flower teaches Wang Lung a new kind of love — "a sickness which is greater than any a man can have." Though he constantly desires her, and though "he went in to her and he had his will of her again and again . . . he came away unsatisfied."

As Pearl Buck states it: "there was no health in her for him." All else is subordinated to his love for her. He does not care for Ching's reports of the fields and the receding waters. He spends much of his time taking baths, which contrasts to the ritual bath he took before meeting O-lan, and he even has his braid cut off in order to please Lotus Flower; in contrast to Lotus, O-lan thinks that her husband has cut off his life.

The analogy between Wang and Hwang is drawn for us by O-lan who, in a tone of scorn, says, "There is that about you which makes me think of one of the lords in the great house." Naturally, Wang Lung, in his present state of mind, takes this as a compliment. And much like the reports that we have of the members of the House of Hwang, Wang Lung lets the silver freely pass through his hands, spending it on jewels and favors for Lotus. Naturally, too, the relationship between Wang Lung and O-lan suffers during this period. O-lan is afraid to speak to him, knowing that his anger is always ready for a woman who "clearly had no beauty of hair or of person." The final insult by Wang Lung is when he takes the two pearls that O-lan has saved between her breasts; he plans to give them to Lotus, stating that "pearls are for fair women!"

CHAPTERS 20-21

These two chapters continue with the love that possesses Wang Lung. It is, however, modified by the arrival of Wang Lung's uncle. In China, where ancestor worship is the main type of worship, Wang Lung resents his uncle and his uncle's intrusion, but he knows also that "it is a shame to a man when he has enough and spare to drive his own father's brother and son from the house." Consequently, Wang Lung now has three more people living in the house.

Wang Lung himself, cannot quench his passion for Lotus Flower and does not know what to do next, as he is consumed in his love for this dainty person. The solution comes, ironically, from his uncle's wife, whom he overhears talking to O-lan. The uncle's wife sees immediately what no one else has observed — that Wang Lung is having an affair with another woman. When she casually mentions that someone as wealthy as Wang Lung has every right to buy a concubine, the solution to Wang Lung's problem becomes obvious: he will buy Lotus Flower and keep her as his concubine. Wang Lung even relies on his uncle's wife to complete all the transactions, while he sees to the building of another court that will house Lotus Flower and Cuckoo. He even builds goldfish ponds and buys delicate food.

The contrast between the earlier arrival of O-lan (and her big feet) walking behind Wang Lung and the arrival of Lotus Flower in a closed sedan chair is interesting. Without O-lan, Wang Lung would never have been able to afford his concubine at this stage of his life, and yet his main attraction to Lotus Flower is her small feet, which are so delicate that she cannot stand on them for a long period of time; she walks "tottering and swaying upon her little feet and leaning upon Cuckoo." Thus Chapter 20 concentrates upon Wang Lung's all-consuming passion for Lotus Flower.

Chapter 21 shows this passion being somewhat abated — at least to the point that it does not totally occupy Wang Lung's life. And, whereas he expected trouble from O-lan about the arrival of Lotus Flower, his main trouble comes as a result of the presence of Cuckoo. O-lan dismisses Lotus Flower with a single comment: "and to that one you gave my two pearls"; however, she cannot abide the concept that Cuckoo is in her house because Cuckoo was a slave in the House of Hwang and ordered O-lan about and constantly insulted her. O-lan's hatred is so great that she will not even boil water for Cuckoo; thus Wang

Lung has to build a separate kitchen for Lotus Flower and Cuckoo.

Wang Lung's love begins to cool when he first discovers that Lotus Flower likes his uncle's wife and doesn't want him to come to her when the uncle's wife is visiting with her: "his love cooled a little, although he did not know it himself . . . and so his love for Lotus was not whole and perfect as it had been before, absorbing utterly his mind and his body."

When the twins take the "fool" into Lotus Flower's court and she screams at them, Wang Lung becomes angry at her for the first time and "he was most angry of all that Lotus Flower dared to curse this child of his" because throughout the novel, he seems to have very special feelings for his "fool," fearing for her as he approaches death at the end of the novel.

Wang Lung is not completely comfortable with Lotus Flower and is somewhat ashamed when his ancient father discovers her in one of the courts and screams out that there is a "harlot in the house." Until the death of O-lan, and even afterward, he has twinges of conscience about his relationship with Lotus Flower, even though this was a perfectly acceptable situation for a man of Wang Lung's standing (see section on Concubinage).

At the end of the chapter, Wang Lung has recovered enough from his love for Lotus Flower to be able to take his hoe and go into the fields to work, symbolizing the healing power of the earth for him.

CHAPTERS 22-24

After Wang Lung has somewhat abated his infatuation for Lotus Flower, he is able to return to the land and he is "healed of his sickness of love by the good dark earth . . . soft as black sugar . . . and the health of the earth spread into his flesh and he was healed of his sickness." Again, Pearl Buck is emphasizing

the powers of the "good earth" to heal Wang Lung and to re-
mind the reader that, when one loses close contact with the
"good earth," one is in danger of losing contact with the good
qualities of life itself. For example, Wang Lung goes out and eats
garlic, an act which would immediately identify him as a plain
farmer and a crude person. Yet he laughs about it and decides
that he can eat whatever he likes. He is no longer dismayed
that people smell garlic on his breath and refer to him in derogatory terms because he is "full of health again and free of the
sickness of his love."

As is fitting for a man of Wang Lung's wealth, he is now established in his own rank so that he can place his women in their
proper positions — Lotus is his concubine who is to give him
pleasure in bed and O-lan is his wife who has borne him children
so as to continue the line of the House of Wang. Also, note that
Wang Lung has always been a person who is concerned about
the opinion of other people; now, he takes pleasure that the
men of the town are talking about him and come to him to hear
his opinion about various matters and accept his decisions. Furthermore, he is pleased that the men of the town admire him
because he has sufficient money to have a concubine for his own
pleasure and to have his sons educated so that they can read and
write the Chinese characters.

Chapter 22 also informs the reader that the House of Wang
is becoming an important and influential house since even O-lan
notes that the eldest son is acting much like one of the young
lords in the old House of Hwang, where she was a slave. This
attests to the rise of Wang Lung: his wife, who was once a slave,
is now the mother of sons who conduct themselves like young
lords. The young people are growing further and further away
from the "good earth."

As Wang Lung recognizes that his son is acting like a young
lord, he decides to marry him off quickly. At first, he cannot
understand why his son acts as he does because he knows that
he himself never had such desires. Then he remembers that he
never had any leisure time; he worked constantly and, therefore,
never had the time to develop lascivious desires.

When Wang Lung mentions his eldest son's problem to Lotus Flower, she tells of a grain merchant in town who has a suitable daughter. She then says that Cuckoo knows all things and, when Cuckoo is called, we learn that it is Liu, the grain dealer to whom Wang Lung has always sold his grain. Cuckoo wants to arrange the entire affair since there will be a handsome fee involved.

To make matters worse, Wang Lung finds out that the uncle's son has been taking Wang Lung's eldest son to see a prostitute, Yang, and Wang Lung goes to her and promises her twice her fee if she refuses to see his son again. Wang Lung is now determined to throw his uncle out of his house, but when he confronts him, the uncle shows Wang Lung an undershirt which depicts a read beard and, immediately, Wang Lung knows that his uncle is an important official with the local group of marauding bandits. He realizes that if he throws his uncle out he will be pillaged by this group; the only reason that he has enjoyed relative safety these past few years is because his uncle has protected him. Thus, he is trapped into giving further protection and boarding to his uncle and his family. At this point, Wang Lung, "when the affairs of his house became too deep for him, he took a hoe and went to his fields." He became healthy again through contact with the "good earth." For that same season, he had to endure the attack of a brood of swarming locusts, but some of his crops survived and, in the meantime, Wang Lung is concerned only with his land. All else is unimportant to him.

The eldest son now wants to continue his education in the southern part of China. Wang Lung feels that his son knows enough for this part of the country. His desire to go south is correlated with Lotus Flower who, we learn later, has been talking to the son, even though she pretends that it is Cuckoo who has given her the information. O-lan, who rarely says anything, reports to Wang Lung that she thinks that the eldest son goes too often into the inner courts. Wang Lung then sets a trap to see if the eldest son does indeed go into the inner courts where Lotus lives. When he discovers the truth, he beats the son unmercifully.

To the Western reader, this act might seem strange, but in Chinese law, the father is the supreme authority and, if a son raised his hand against a father, the son could be put to death. Also for the first time, Wang Lung beats Lotus Flower, an act which creates a definite change between the two people.

CHAPTERS 25-26

With the eldest son gone, Wang Lung feels greatly relieved, as if "the house was purged of some surcharge of unrest." After the experience with the eldest son, Wang Lung resolves to quickly take the second son out of school and to apprentice him to a trade.

To the relief of Wang Lung, his second son is greatly different from the eldest. This difference will be clearer later in the novel, when the second son is very practical and mercenary, and the eldest, who is partly influenced by his wife, prefers opulence and extravagance.

Wang Lung arranges the apprenticeship of the second son to the grain merchant, the father of the eldest son's betrothed and, while there, Wang Lung also talks of arranging a second bond of the families by betrothing his ten-year-old daughter to Liu's ten-year-old son. A final discussion must wait, however, for "it was not a thing that could be discussed face to face beyond this."

On returning home, Wang Lung thinks of the possible betrothal of his second daughter. He is pleased to reflect on his daughter's beauty and the fact that her mother had bound her feet "so that she moved about with graceful steps." But he is sad to find that the bindings are very painful and make her cry and lose sleep. (See section on foot-binding.)

Most of all, he is moved by her confession that her mother told her not to cry at night, nor bother Wang Lung with her pain, for she must endure the pain of foot-binding or her husband some day will not love her, even as Wang Lung does not love O-lan. For the first time in years, with all of his children provided for, and a tie with the land established in his youngest son, Wang Lung begins to think of O-lan as the faithful servant which she has been to him.

His new regard for O-lan causes him to realize that the "fire in her vitals" is now causing her great pain. His new feeling for her moves him to force her to go to bed while he goes for a doctor.

The call by the doctor illustrates the custom of physicians in China — a tradition that carried on from the earliest dynasties; that is, a doctor is paid a set fee to keep a patient well. Loss of that patient is punishable by law; this liability holds until the patient is fully recovered. In this case, the doctor sees that there is no hope for O-lan, so rather than admitting that he does not have the ability to save her and, rather than speak of her death in front of O-lan and Wang Lung, the doctor sets a prohibitive fee. This fee, in effect, says, "the woman will die."

In the following chapter, we see the custom of coffin buying. Wang Lung buys the coffin for O-lan and tells her of it to show her that she will be provided for after her death. It is also interesting to note that Wang Lung does some "bargain shopping" at the coffin-maker's shop. Knowing that his father is soon to die and, informed that by buying two coffins, he can get a discount off the price of two, Wang Lung buys two coffins.

The sickness of O-lan is greatly felt in the house: the house becomes messy, the old man misses O-lan in his senility, and Wang Lung now has to care for the "poor fool." And the whole time, he thinks of O-lan and what her loss means. He tells her that he would sell all of his land to save her life, but she is ready for death and points out that the land is more permanent than life, for she must die eventually, but the land will always be there after her.

Having seen her coffin, O-lan is more content to die because, in the Chinese custom, a person who can be buried in an expensive coffin is a more honorable person than one who is simply thrown into the ground without the benefit of a coffin. Thus, O-lan knows that she is dying as one who began as a slave, but has ended her life as the wife of a prominent man, and who has borne that man sons. As O-lan says to Cuckoo on her death bed: "Well, and you may have lived in the courts of the Old Lord, and you were accounted beautiful, but I have been a man's wife and I have borne him sons, and you are still a slave."

Due to her resentment of Cuckoo, O-lan will feel more comfort on her deathbed if she can see her son married and her daughter-in-law in charge of the household, particularly the kitchen, and also know that she will continue to live in the sons of her sons.

After the death of O-lan, Wang Lung goes to the geomancer —a person who is not necessarily a figure of any religion, but is mostly aligned to superstitions. Then he goes to priests of the Taoist temple, then to the Buddhist temple, thus indicating that Wang Lung's religion, if indeed it may be called a religion, is a mixture of several different beliefs. The final emphasis of the chapter, however, is that, in this good earth, is "buried the first good half of my life and more." This emphasizes again Wang Lung's close association with and reliance upon the "good earth."

CHAPTERS 27-28

These chapters continue to show how Wang Lung becomes a wealthy and powerful man. This is accomplished as a result of several factors. First, a great flood comes at a time when Wang Lung had given over the entire management to Ching and "had scarcely thought whether [he] had land or not these days except to bury the dead in." As Wang Lung goes out to inspect the land, he again curses the evil of the gods. This frightens Ching, who seems to be more in awe of the gods than Wang Lung.

As the waters cover the land, famine sets in. There is only a small portion of the land that can be planted. And as the waters remain, there is no chance to plant land for the next season and "everywhere people starved and were hungry and were angry at what had befallen them." When the waters do not recede in time to plant the wheat for winter, it is evident that there will be no harvest next year. For the first time in ages, Wang Lung takes control and begins to ration out what is needed for the household. Only to Lotus Flower will he allow more than the bare essentials.

Wang Lung, however, has more wealth than most people suspect: there is silver hid in many places about the house. And he is able to deceive everyone—except his uncle. Wang Lung is constantly annoyed that he is under such strict obligations to his uncle because he knows that if it had not been for his uncle's power with the robbers that his house would have been ransacked long ago. Never has he so resented having to give out silver. The resentment is so strong that the eldest son suggests they drown the uncle. But Wang Lung is a very honorable man and cannot tolerate such an act. They discover a ploy whereby they will keep the uncle and his wife there but will render them helpless—they will buy opium for them and, once addicted, neither will be a nuisance. This decision points out that once one is a great family corruption begins to enter in. We should remember the description of the Ancient Mistress when Wang Lung went to get O-lan. She was literally consumed by opium, as eventually the uncle and his wife will be.

After the uncle's son tries to attack Wang Lung's youngest daughter, he goes to see Liu, the grain merchant to whose son the daughter is promised, and tells him: "Since she is to be your family, let her virginity be guarded here." This fact further demonstrates the insignificant position of women in the Chinese family. After Wang Lung takes his thirteen-year-old daughter to Liu's house, he never sees her again for the rest of his life, even though they live only a short distance across town. Furthermore, he rarely thinks of her.

After freeing himself of his anxiety for his youngest daughter, he turns his attention to solving his next problem—the uncle and the uncle's wife. He approaches the problem in a most casual manner, bringing opium to them and off-handedly saying that it is only a little something that he once bought for his own ailing father. As they become addicted, Wang Lung does not object to the silver which he has to spend because it brings him peace of mind—the one thing he has desired throughout his lifetime.

This use of opium also represents one of the final phases in the establishment of the House of Wang as a powerful house. As the waters recede, people return to the land and Wang Lung loans some money at great interest rates, and he sells seeds at great profits, and he buys land "dirt cheap." In one day, he buys five slaves because he is a rich man and can now afford it. All are about twelve years old and fully capable of doing good work around the courts. Then, a few days later, he buys a seven-year-old girl because he is touched by "her pretty frightened eyes and her piteous thinness." This girl is Pear Blossom; she will be the last person to share his bed. Thus the House of Wang becomes powerful through the acquisition of more land, more profits, and the addition of six slaves to its courts.

With all of the above good fortune, Wang Lung expects to find peace in his house, but he does not and, again, it is because of his uncle's son and his own eldest son. The original antagonism caused by the uncle's son peeping at the eldest son's wife is still the basic cause of the trouble. Now the cousin also walks around the new slaves improperly attired. The eldest son feels this is a negative reflection upon the rising House of Wang, which is now gradually moving away from the land and into prominence. As he tells Wang Lung, his cousin's conduct "is unseemly in my father's house."

The solution to the problem, according to the eldest son, is for the immediate family to move into town, particularly into the inner courts of the House of Hwang, knowing the effect this will have on his father. The mere mention of this great house causes Wang Lung to remember how he trembled and how he could barely talk the first time he entered. Now he ponders how he "could sit on that seat where the old one sat and from whence she bade me stand like a serf, and now I could sit there and so call another into my presence." Thus, Wang Lung's ultimate decision to move to the House of Hwang is not caused by his eldest son's wishes or the actions of his uncle's son, but because he feels greatness in a place where he once felt so completely subdued.

When Wang Lung consults his second son, this son is pleased the move will allow him to marry and move into the family home. However, the contrast between the two sons is again emphasized as the second son wants a wife who is completely different from the wife of the eldest son.

Astounded at his second son and also pleased with him, Wang Lung goes to look at the old House of Hwang and, upon inspection, decides to rent it. Now Wang Lung is rapidly approaching the position held by the Old Lord at the beginning of the novel — the head of the most powerful house of the province.

CHAPTERS 29-30

Wang Lung is impatient to get the task of moving accomplished. Yet on the day set aside for moving, he is still reluctant to leave the land. Thus, Pearl Buck suggests that, even in wealth, Wang Lung's ties with the land are still exceptionally strong. He resolves to move to his new court before his grandson is born, realizing that he can return to his old home any time he wants to. Later, in the final chapter of the novel, he does return to the land, accompanied by little Pear Blossom.

The moving order of the family carries some significance. As long as O-lan was alive, Lotus Flower was still second to her. Now that O-lan is dead, Lotus Flower has been raised in status; consequently, she and her servant Cuckoo and their slaves are the first to be moved, followed by the eldest son and his wife.

With the help of Ching, whom Wang Lung relies upon more and more, a maid is found for the second son and the wedding is arranged. Now Wang Lung feels that he might have peace since there is only one more son to marry. Thus, as he sleeps in the sun, Pearl Buck shows us how he resembles his father in the beginning of the novel. We have nearly come full circle.

Now that Ching is getting older and there is so much land to look after, Wang Lung decides to rent portions of the land and take half of the crops in lieu of rent. Wang Lung is becoming more and more like the Old Lord of the House of Hwang, who merely sat in his courts with his mistresses and collected his rents.

When the uncle's son comes and asks for money in order to join the war in the North, Wang Lung finally discovers peace for himself. He now has enough money to do anything he wants; there seems to be peace and tranquility, and he "who once had been well satisfied with good wheaten bread wrapped about a stick of garlic" now eats "dainty foods" and dresses his slaves better than he himself was dressed in his youth. He is especially pleased when Cuckoo refers to him as "a lord."

When it comes time for his eldest son's wife to give birth, Wang Lung again goes to the gods—promising nice things if it is to be a boy, but threatening to forsake them if it is a girl.

More important, however, is the contrast in this scene between the birth of Wang Lung's eldest son and the birth of this grandson. Wang Lung remembers how O-lan refused help from anyone, gave birth to the child alone, and then came back to the fields to help with the harvest. In contrast, this daughter-in-law "cried like a child with her pains," and she had "the slaves running in the house, and her husband there by her door." The contrast makes Wang Lung realize how old he is because the memories of O-lan are like vague dreams.

The birth of the grandson is paralleled by the death of Ching—a death which affects him more than did the death of his own father. Ching had been with Wang Lung so long, even at the meager wedding feast for O-lan, and had served Wang Lung so well that he wants to bury Ching in the family burial plot where his father and O-lan are buried. But the eldest son is horrified at such an indiscretion that Wang Lung relents and buries Ching farther down the hill. Now is the time to make a complete separation from the land: he rents his land out and takes his "fool" and youngest son to town. Now the family has completely dissolved its closeness with the "good earth."

But there is not yet peace, for Wang Lung longs only to lounge in the sun, and the eldest son harangues him about acquiring all the outer courts. He even holds his nose as he walks through the rabble which inhabits the outer courts. Wang Lung agrees, and the eldest son begins to refurbish and redecorate the outer courts befitting a family whom the townspeople now call "the great House of Wang." A conflict occurs, however, when the second son resents all the money being spent simply to impress people. When Wang Lung finds out that the wedding preparations will cost ten times the price of the bride, he orders the elder son to desist.

Next, Wang Lung is plagued by the youngest son, who does not want to stay on the land but wants to be educated as were his older brothers. It troubles Wang Lung that he has no son upon the land but, in order to have peace, he has a tutor engaged to teach the youngest son.

As the years pass, Wang Lung, in the space of five years, has five grandsons and three granddaughters and each child has his own individual slave when it is born. Thus the House of Wang is becoming not only a powerful house, but a very large house.

After the ravages of opium, Wang Lung's uncle is on the verge of death and the uncle's wife hopes that if their son comes home that Wang Lung will find a bride suitable for him so that he might carry on the family name. When the uncle dies, Wang Lung has the uncle's wife brought to the great house in town. She is now as dried and yellow as was the Old Mistress whom Wang Lung had once feared so greatly.

CHAPTERS 31-32

Wang Lung, who has now lived through more than one drought and more than one flood, swarms of locusts, famines, and other disasters, has never seen a war. The mere fact that he refers to the war as something to be seen re-establishes the fact that he is a simple peasant from the "good earth." The second son advises him not to sell his grain because with the war approaching, they will be able to get a better price. Thus, after having lived through all the other calamities of life and having reached a respected position in society, Wang Lung now must suffer the indignities of having to quarter numerous soldiers who swarmed "out of the northwest like a swarm of locusts."

When Wang Lung first sees the soldiers, he does not even know what the implement is that they carry over their shoulders, and the faces of the men are so fierce that he wants to hurry inside and lock the gates. But before he can do this, the uncle's son sees him and has all of his horde of men move into Wang Lung's courts. Thus again is the uncle's son a source of evil to Wang Lung.

When the second son arrives with reports of how the soldiers will kill a person for the slightest provocation, Wang Lung and his sons realize the seriousness of the matter and immediately move all the women and children into the inner courts. They guard these courts against the soldiers, but in the same way that they could not deny the uncle anything because of family or ancestral ties, so now they must let the uncle's son into their innermost courts, where he insults the wife of the eldest son and makes sexual insinuations with the wife of the second son—a fact that will cause great enmity between the two women.

The uncle's son becomes so obnoxious concerning the females that they decide that it will be necessary to give him a woman while he is there. He chooses the delicate Pear Blossom, the slave whom Wang Lung bought when she was seven years old because she looked so pitiful. He has always felt tender toward her and, when she falls to her feet begging him not to send her, he searches for another woman or another way to satisfy the uncle's son.

A good healthy slave girl, twenty years old, volunteers and, for the moon and a half before the uncle's son and the horde of soldiers are called away, he "had the wench" at his will and left after she had conceived by him. Wang Lung was thankful it was only a girl because if it had been a male, then, according to Chinese custom, it would have had a permanent place in the House of Wang.

Wang Lung and his sons agree that every trace of the destruction caused by the soldiers must be removed. Also, being kind-hearted, he tells the slave girl that she can have the room of the uncle's wife who is about to die. Instead, she asks to be wed to a farmer, since she has grown accustomed to having a man in her bed. Thus, as soon as the uncle's wife is dead, the slave asks Wang Lung to find her a farmer. Now the story has come full circle because Wang Lung calls the stout fellow who helped Ching and offers him the girl whom he is glad to have because she is stout and can help in the fields. Now Wang Lung sits on his dias and gives instructions—whereas once he stood before this very dias receiving instructions. And whereas he received a stout woman from this house, he is now giving a poor farmer, as he was once a poor farmer, a stout young girl. Whether or not this young couple will flourish as well as did Wang Lung and O-lan is outside the speculations of Pearl Buck's story. Instead, she is emphasizing how Wang Lung himself has completed a cycle in life.

Wang Lung, however, has one last problem before he finds peace in his life. Lotus Flower, who has grown fat and unattractive, accuses Wang Lung of having an affair with little Pear Blossom since he protected her from the uncle's son. Actually, the idea has never occurred to Wang Lung until Lotus Flower mentions it. Then, as he noticed the pretty little slave, something stirs within his loins.

At this time, too, Wang Lung is troubled by another son. The youngest son wants to go away and be a soldier. He has apparently talked with all the soldiers quartered in the house and has heard how they are fighting to free the land. Even though Pearl Buck never says it, all the implications are that these soldiers are part of the Communist forces. Wang Lung has been horrified to hear his youngest son talk in such a way about the land which has always been so sacred to him. But now that he is rich, he offers his son the choice of schools in the South or even the choice of one of the slaves as his mistress. This second offer shows how far Wang Lung has departed from his old ways as a farmer, when he condemned young lords for taking any slave at their whim. Now Wang Lung is doing the same thing until the youngest son maintains that none of the slaves are even worth looking at—unless it is Pear Blossom. A sudden jealousy is aroused in Wang Lung and he is left confused.

CHAPTERS 33-34

Wang Lung cannot free himself from the thought of the youthful beauty of Pear Blossom, and he is ashamed since he is approaching seventy years old. One day, however, as she passes him, he calls her forth and she, feeling "from him the heat of his blood," confesses that she cannot stand the fiery passions of young men and much prefers to have old men who are gentle. He leads her to his own courts, where she then becomes his last concubine—one who will be with him until the end of his life and will look after his needs until death.

In Chinese custom, it is understood that a great lord can have his choice of women in his house and it is not a shame to him or his family. Yet Wang Lung does feel shame because this is contrary to the way in which he spent his childhood—having early learned to frown on the decadent ways of the great rich families. Yet here he is free to do all the things that great rich lords do. He is even afraid to face Lotus Flower, though he has not been with her for years. He bribes Cuckoo to tell Lotus Flower that Pear Blossom is moving in with him.

He is next concerned about what his sons will say. The second son learns of Pear Blossom first and says nothing. Then the eldest son, who is always more finicky, is at first incredulous but finally dismisses it with the remark: "you are rich and you may do as you like." When the youngest son comes in that night and discovers Pear Blossom with his father, he "gleams" at his father, conveying a sense of moral indignation. He then announces with a fierce, low, and surcharged voice: "Now I will go for a soldier." There is the sense that this son is the one who is breaking from the ancient Chinese customs which allow such absolute sovereignty to the reigning male. The youngest son is ready to fight to give more rights to females — as did Pearl Buck — when she herself worked in a house for refugee slaves fleeing cruel masters.

Being an old man, Wang Lung's passion "died out of him"; yet he is still fond of Pear Blossom. In fact, she is the only one he trusts to look after his "poor fool" after he is dead. He gives Pear Blossom some powder which will kill the "poor fool" and so that she will follow Wang Lung in death. Pear Blossom objects that she cannot even kill an insect and promises to look after the "fool" after Wang Lung is dead. "Wang Lung trusted her and was comforted for the fate of his poor fool."

Wang Lung is now so old that he does not even know what his own family is doing and has to inquire of Cuckoo about the nature of his family, and he learns that he now has eleven grandsons and eight granddaughters. But the one thing that never leaves Wang Lung is his love for the land, for the good earth. "He had gone away from it and he had set up his house in a town and he was rich. But his roots were in his land." As he feels death drawing near, he asks his eldest son to get him a coffin and bring it to the earthen house where he will move and end his days where he was born. Taking Pear Blossom, his fool, and a few servants, he returns to the good earth which brought about the establishment of the House of Wang. Once when the eldest and second son come for a visit, he overhears them talking of selling the land and he firmly resists such talk: "Out of the land we came and into it we must go — and if you will hold your land you can live—no one can rob you of land." Consequently, from our first glimpse of Wang Lung on his wedding day, when he felt as one with the good earth and through all his trials, he hung onto his land to the very end; Wang Lung has constantly emphasized his alliance with the "good earth."

CHARACTER ANALYSES

WANG LUNG

From the first time we encounter Wang Lung until our final view of him, his main concern is the "good earth" and the sustenance that it gives. When we first meet him, preparing for his wedding day, he takes his bath water and returns it to the good earth. We also discover that his house and his gods are both made from the good earth. He is presented as a simple peasant farmer, one who is so frightened in front of the Ancient Mistress of the House of Hwang that he cannot speak. Even in the fields, he is a very silent person, and we seldom get to know little of what he is thinking inwardly. Thus our knowledge of him comes from the author's journalistic style.

In the early parts of the book, Wang Lung is quiet; he is content to eat no more than some garlic wrapped around some unleavened bread, but by the end of the book, when he has established his family as one of the great families, he prefers more "dainty foods" and is able to pick and choose among his foods.

Throughout the novel, Wang Lung is never able to escape the fact or belief that all good things come from the good earth and that all things are ultimately returned to it. Whenever he has a piece of silver, he knows that the silver can be stolen from him, but if he is able to invest the silver into good land, then no one can steal the land from him. This is illustrated when he has to go South during a period of great famine; when he returns, his land is still there, even though all other things, even the hinges on his door, are stolen.

As soon as he discovers that O-lan has the costly jewels, he wants immediately to invest them in good land. With the deaths of various members of his family, he knows that they are returning to the land from whence they came. When it comes time for him to die, he goes back to the "earth house" where he was born and has his coffin delivered to the earth house, where he will wait to return to the "good earth."

O-LAN

O-lan is as basic as Wang Lung. On her wedding day, when she humbly follows Wang Lung home, she is seen as a model, in some ways, of the perfect Chinese wife. She is humble and subservient; in fact, she is so quiet that Wang Lung never knows what she is thinking. However, she is so resourceful that Wang Lung is constantly surprised at her ability to adapt to all new situations. For example, she knows how to make a shanty out of mats and, when the big mansion is raided, she knows where the rich lords might likely keep their jewels.

Part of her strength and resourcefulness is seen when she delivers her own children. At the birth of the first child, she works in the fields with Wang Lung until it is time for the birth. She asks only for a sharp reed in order to cut the child's "life from mine." Immediately after the birth, she returns to the fields to help with the harvest. This contrasts greatly with the delivery of Wang Lung's first grandchild, who causes a great disturbance in the great house before it is delivered.

To understand the contrast between the humility of O-lan in the first part of the novel and the stoic abilities of O-lan at the end of the novel, we have to re-evaluate the situation. The pride we see in O-lan in the later chapters of the novel can be traced to having been brought up as a slave and abused in a great house and rising to become Wang Lung's wife with sons of her own. This is more important to her than physical beauty.

THE CHINESE CUSTOM OF FOOT-BINDING

The Chinese custom of binding a young girl's feet plays an important role in *The Good Earth*. When Wang Lung first sees O-lan, he immediately notes that her feet are not bound; later, he has O-lan bind his daughter's feet. He becomes disgusted with O-lan's feet and he is attracted to Lotus partly because of her bound feet. The practice of foot-binding symbolized many things to the Chinese man. To Wang Lung, it symbolizes, among other things, the aristocratic society from which he was excluded.

In a society so old, so large, and so diverse as that of China, it is impossible to accurately trace the origin of such a custom. There are many stories concerning the origin of this custom and perhaps part of each story has some element of truth. Most authorities claim that the practice started during the T'ang dynasty (618-907 A.D.). One of the earliest stories asserts that bound feet originally came from the practice of wearing bow-shoes. These were small shoes with upturned toes and were worn by royal dancers in the royal court. A poet-king (Li Yu) thought fancifully that the dancers would dance more gracefully if their feet were bound in cloth. Consequently, he made his favorite dancer dance with her feet bound in cloth which was then decorated with pearls and precious stones so as to resemble lotus flowers. The poet-king then wrote verses about the beauty of the dancer's feet, calling them "little golden lotus flowers" or, sometimes, "little golden lilies." Thus because of the beautiful verses written by the king, binding of the feet became a popular and fashionable thing throughout the kingdom. "Lotus" was often another name for bound feet and, thus, Wang Lung's concubine is appropriately named "Lotus."

Another story concerns another king in the T'ang dynasty. This king's concubine decided to have her feet bound in order to make herself more desirable in the king's eyes. The king was so pleased with her attempts to please him and with the beauty of her small feet that the other ladies of the court soon followed the concubine's example in order to please the king.

A third story involves an empress (Tak-ki) during the Shang dynasty. She had club feet and was very ashamed of them and was also jealous of the other women in the court. Consequently, she forced all other women to bind their feet so that they too would become deformed.

A final story deals with political power. An emperor had trouble keeping his wife out of political matters. To keep her from interfering in matters of state, he had her feet and the feet of her followers bound so that she was forced to remain in her quarters. This final story conforms with the Chinese male's suppression of his woman. Because the woman could walk only a very short distance, she was confined primarily to her household. It would therefore be a disgrace for a woman to show her face beyond the doors of her home. Of course, with her feet bound, the woman was quite content to remain at home because, in addition to the pain of walking on them, she could not balance herself for a long period of time; consequently, she had no desire to do anything that would take an extra amount of energy.

All of the above stories have one thing in common—each deals with royalty. Thus it is safe to assume that the practice actually did start with someone of royal blood. The practice can then be related to royalty, sophistication, and social prestige. To do what the king did would elevate the average Chinese man's estimate of himself.

The binding of feet, if done properly, was started when the girl was five or six years old. The feet were bound by yards of cloth that would not stretch. To start the process, the foot was extended at the ankle, and the fleshy part of the heel was pushed down and forward under the foot. The foot was then carefully wound up with the material. The tight binding primarily cut the circulation, and this retarded the growth of the foot. It is easy to see that the toes would become bent under the pressure and would not spread out to their normal width. The binding would force the foot to become narrow and tapering. After a while, the toes would stay curled under, even when the bandages were removed for cleaning and changing.

Women's feet would then have unnaturally prominent insteps as a result of this process. If done properly, the heel would become elongated and grow down to the ground level—that is, it would be on the same level as the bent-under large toe. Essentially, then, the woman walked on her toes and heels, the whole foot being about four or five inches in length. The entire process could take several years before all growth was arrested.

The shoe to fit this foot was somewhat smaller than the foot —about three or four inches in length. Part of the heel stuck out of the shoe and it was tied to the outside by a piece of cloth. The woman would wear thin cloth around the foot inside the shoe. On the outside, thicker cloth was wound around the ankle. The girls not only made their shoes themselves, but they also embroidered them with various designs. The design of the shoes was considered part of the accomplishment of a young woman.

The difficulty of the above legends concerning the origin of the custom is that if the feet were not bound while the child was young, it was almost impossible to do so after she had reached maturity. After twelve years of age, the foot would be about as big as it would ever get. When feet were bound at an older age, the only thing that usually happened was that the toes curled under. The heel would never grow down to toe level, and a wooden block had to be placed under the heel for support.

As with Wang Lung's daughter, who wept from the pain of her bindings when her mother tightened the bandages too tightly, it is easy to see that the entire process was a very painful one. Often the skin and flesh broke and cracked if too much pressure was applied or if the feet of an older girl were bound. If sores appeared, they were difficult to heal. The bandages had to remain on if the process was to work because of the necessity of constant pressure. Many times infection and gangrene set in and many times the girl would die from the procedure. Thus, we have the old Chinese saying: "For every pair of small feet, there is a jar full of tears."

One would think that such an unnatural and painful process would be quickly abolished, but, instead, it became a part of

Chinese culture. Books were written on properly formed feet, and men praised the ones that were properly formed. Poets traveled to different areas of China to compare feet, and emperors went to the southern provinces for sexual indulgences since women in the South were famous for their small feet. Women continued the practice until well into the twentieth century, for, next to a good face, a woman was immeasurably proud of her small feet. Even though the bound feet were unmercifully painful, yet if she had a well-shaped pair, it was her pride for life.

As noted above, besides being a mark of gentility and indulgence, bound feet were thought to be seductive. Men thought that if a girl bound her feet, her waist became more slender, and her breasts and hips bigger and more shapely. In his book *My Country and My People*, Lin Yutang writes that "small feet influenced the whole carriage and walking gait of the woman, throwing the hips backward, and effecting an extremely gingerly gait, the body "shimmying" all over. Looking at a woman with bound feet walking was like looking at a rope-dancer, tantalizing to the highest degree." The bound feet, then, were some of the highest sophistications of the Chinese sensual imagination.

In Wang Lung's case, it was a mere indulgence to have a woman with bound feet. She was almost useless; she could not work in the fields or carry heavy loads, as O-lan did. She was kept as a "toy" to show other men that the master of the house could feed a mouth that did not work for its pay. The possession of Lotus by Wang Lung causes the villagers to respect him more. It shows that he is rich enough to afford his pleasures; he does not worry where his next meal is coming from.

Thus as Wang Lung becomes wealthier, foot-binding takes on more significance to him. Even though he noted on their first meeting that O-lan had big feet, yet during the years of work, this fact did not bother him. When he has more money and leisure, however, he looks at O-lan and "she was altogether hideous, but the most hideous of all were her big feet in their loose cotton cloth shoes." Now that he has money, Wang Lung begins to realize that something is lacking in his life. It is then that he discovers the concubine Lotus, and his attraction for her is based, in part, on her small feet.

When Wang Lung moves Lotus into his house and builds her own separate court, she never goes out. One reason for this is simply that she cannot walk very far on her bound feet. She is kept like a toy or a pet, one who is expected to serve no other function than being a sex object.

Wang Lung's change in attitude is also shown in his view of his daughter. He makes O-lan bind the girl's feet so that they can enable her to find a good husband. Thus even Wang Lung, basically a mere farmer, represents the Chinese's long tradition of considering small feet to be associated with elegance and royalty.

LOTUS FLOWER AND CONCUBINAGE

There are few Westerners who can understand the Chinese practice of concubinage as it was practiced up until the 1930s. In actuality, the practice of concubinage is a logical outgrowth of the Chinese family structure, particularly as it applied to the position of women in the Chinese family, in which the male was the supreme authority.

As a daughter, a Chinese girl had no rights at all. In fact, the birth of a female child was considered to be both a time of sadness and a time of an evil omen, as we see when Wang Lung considers the birth of his daughters to be signs that the gods are not favoring him. No celebration is held if a girl is born: Wang Lung even threatens the gods at the birth of his first grandchild. A female child was considered to be a liability to the family because she was thought to be only a temporary member of the family — someone who had to be supported until she could be married. And since she was married at an early age, she could never perform enough work in order to pay for the expenses for her years in the family. Wang Lung gives his daughter away when she is thirteen because he can no longer guarantee her virginity. After she leaves him, Wang Lung never sees her again. Also, in poor families, a daughter could be sold as a slave to a rich man; O-lan, for example, was sold when she was a young girl and Wang Lung is even tempted to sell his "fool." Note, too, that Wang Lung, when he becomes rich, buys "slaves" (girls from poor families) for all the members of his household.

Thus, a daughter is trained to become a subservient person to her husband's will and, as a wife, she is constantly expected to obey her husband without question. For example, when Wang Lung discovers that O-lan has a sack of jewels, he asks for them and she obeys without question — except for the bold request to keep two small pearls which she later surrenders to him when he demands them.

A wife can never divorce her husband, but he can divorce her for seven different reasons, some of which are related to concubinage. The seven reasons for divorce are: 1) loquacity, or talking too much. Thus we see throughout the novel that O-lan is naturally reticent and speaks out about something only on rare occasions. 2) An incurable disease. At the end of the novel, when O-lan is dying from a tumor, Wang Lung could divorce her, but the thought never enters his mind. 3) Theft. This does not refer to the type of theft that O-lan committed when she took the jewels from the rich man's house; instead, it means stealing from one's husband or his family. 4) Adultery. Whereas a man can sleep with any woman whom he owns, if a woman ever commits adultery, she is immediately cast out. If a man owns a concubine at the time, then the concubine is elevated to the position of the first wife. 5) Disobedience. When Wang Lung asks for the jewels, O-lan knows that she has to obey her husband because disobedience to him is reason enough for divorce. 6) Jealousy. When Wang Lung brings Lotus Flower into his house, O-lan virtually never complains about her. She does complain about the presence of Cuckoo, but she mentions Lotus Flower only in indirect reference, as when she tells Wang Lung that the eldest son goes too often "into the inner courts." 7) Barrenness. This is by far the most important, the most tantamount, reason for divorce. In Chinese custom, sex is a means of propagating the family name because the family lives through the sons of the family. One of the most sacred, unwritten laws is that ancestors require male descendants. If one woman proves barren, then another woman must be found who can produce male children. If the wife comes from a wealthy family and brings with her many female servants, the wife herself, if barren, offers one of her servants to her husband.

The idea of concubinage dates back to at least the time of Confucius (551?-478? B.C.), who was the father of the religion of ancestor worship and who emphasized in his teachings the importance of male descendants. Consequently, if the wife did not bear male descendants, the man must look to other sources or else violate one of the concepts of Confucianism. Later Confucian scholars expressed the desirability of marrying a wife for her virtues and then taking a concubine for her beauty. Because of the practice of the family's arranging the marriages (Wang Lung's father arranges for Wang Lung's marriage) and because the Chinese man could not see his bride until the wedding day, the later possession of a concubine for her beauty alone was a common practice. If his wife happened to be beautiful, the man could congratulate himself, but if this were not the case, then he could turn elsewhere. Often, the bride's mother, if wealthy, would deliberately select attractive servants (or dowry maids) in the hope that her son-in-law would not have to go outside his own home in search of a sexual mate. Since the dowry maids were a part of the bride's dowry, then, he owned them in the same way as a wealthy man owned the "slaves" he bought. Thus, as with Pear Blossom, it was an accepted practice that the man could have any woman in his household without disgracing himself or his wife. Wang Lung, however, did feel some embarrassment or apprehension about taking Pear Blossom, even though, technically, no one could condemn this act since she was his property.

Although it does not concern *The Good Earth*, another argument for concubinage concerns a wealthy man who has to travel.

The first wife could not under any circumstance leave the house or the responsibilities for running the household, and a man was not expected to practice sexual abstinence during his travels. Thus, a second lady would generally accompany the master and her position took on legal status since she could not be deserted. Even though her position was not equal to that of a wife, yet various formalities were observed on her entrance to the household, and she was deserving of certain rights. If the first wife died, then she was elevated to that position and another lady was acquired to travel with the master.

In most households, there were two types or two kinds of concubines. The first, as noted above, was acquired through legal formalities and occupied a position from responsibility. The second type was purchased from a tea house, as was Lotus Flower. In either case, as with Wang Lung, the possession of a concubine was a sign that a man had wealth and enough money to devote himself to some of the finer refinements and joys of life. Thus the possession of a concubine brought Wang Lung prestige and respect.

The duties of the concubine were quite simple. She existed solely and completely for the entertainment and sexual gratification of her master. She was not expected to perform any household duties or to have any responsibilities other than those of the bed chamber. She was provided usually with a separate court of her own and she was expected to remain in those quarters and always be ready for her master's desires. Whatever power and influence she possessed came solely from her ability to captivate her master and to gain his total favor. This was easy for Lotus Flower since Wang Lung has an all-consuming desire for Lotus Flower. Her beauty, including her small feet, totally captivated him.

In conclusion, a wife was expected to bear male children while the concubine was expected only to please her master. Furthermore, the wife had certain prescribed duties and was in charge of running the household, including the training of the girl children in the proper matters pertaining to managing their

own households. The concubine, however, had no duties —
except to keep herself beautiful and alluring for her master and
to satisfy his every sexual desire.

REVIEW QUESTIONS

1. Consider the roles of "chance" and "change" in the life of the
   Chinese peasant (especially note Chapters 18, 19, and 20),
   as opposed to a cause-and-effect relationship, illustrated in the
   belief by Wang Lung that hard work will have benefits.

2. Consider the relationship between the House of Hwang and
   the family Wang, especially the rise of the Wangs while the
   House of Hwang is disintegrating. Consider, too, the similarity
   shown in the last half of the novel between the two Houses.

3. Pearl Buck won the 1938 Nobel Prize for Literature for what
   the Nobel Prize Committee called "rich and genuine epic
   portrayals of Chinese peasant life, and for masterpieces of
   biography." How is her talent for writing biography reflected
   in her portrayal of Wang Lung and his family?

4. A basic tenet of the novel seems to be that virtue and hard
   work are rewarded. Yet, the riches that are brought back from
   the South (truly a turning point of the novel) are acquired
   through "chance" and trickery. And, at the end of the novel,
   the roots established by Wang Lung will obviously be pulled
   up as the land is sold and divided by the sons. Is this
   consistent?

5. In *The Chinese Novel* (1939), Pearl Buck writes:

   ". . . the novel in China was the peculiar product of the common
   people. And it was solely their property . . . dealing with all which
   interested the people, with legend and with myth, with lore and
   intrigue, with brigands and wars, with everything, indeed, which
   went to make up the life of the people, high and low."

In what ways do the story and style of *The Good Earth,* in their simplicity, offer something for all readers?

6. The success of *The Good Earth* prompted Pearl Buck to write two sequels, which were finally released with *The Good Earth* in a trilogy entitled *House of Earth.* How does *The Good Earth* lend itself to sequels? In what way is the end of *The Good Earth* a beginning? In the end, how does the family Wang compare to the House of Hwang at the beginning of the novel?

SELECTED BIBLIOGRAPHY

BUCK, PEARL. *My Several Worlds.* New York: John Day Co., 1954.

———. *The Chinese Novel.* New York: John Day Co., 1939.

DOYLE, PAUL A. *Pearl S. Buck.* New York: Twayne Publishers, 1965.

HARRIS, THEODORE F. *Pearl S. Buck: A Biography.* New York: John Day Co., 1969-70.

HSIA, C. T. *The Classic Chinese Novel.* New York: Columbia University Press, 1968.

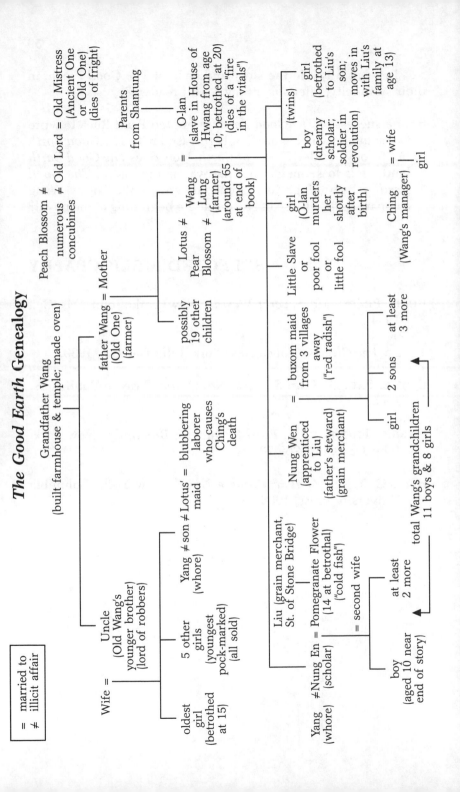

The Good Earth Genealogy

= married to
≠ illicit affair

Grandfather Wang
(built farmhouse & temple; made oven)

Peach Blossom ≠ numerous ≠ Old Lord = Old Mistress
concubines   (Ancient One
                              or Old One)
                              (dies of fright)

Parents
from Shantung

O-lan
(slave in House of
Hwang from age
10; betrothed at 20)
(dies of a "fire
in the vitals")

=

Lotus ≠   Wang Lung
Pear Blossom ≠ (farmer)
               (around 65
               at end of
               book)

father Wang = Mother
(Old One)
(farmer)

possibly
19 other
children

Wife = Uncle
(Old Wang's
younger brother)
(lord of robbers)

oldest
girl
(betrothed
at 15)

5 other
girls
(youngest
pock-marked)
(all sold)

Yang ≠ son ≠ Lotus' = blubbering
(whore)   maid   laborer
                       who causes
                       Ching's death

girl
(betrothed
to Liu's
son;
moves in
with Liu's
family at
age 13)

(twins)

boy
(dreamy
scholar;
soldier in
revolution)

girl
(O-lan
murders
her shortly
after birth)

Little Slave
or poor fool
or little fool

Ching = wife
(Wang's manager)
girl

Nung Wen
(apprenticed
to Liu)
(father's steward)
(grain merchant)

= buxom maid
from 3 villages
away
("red radish")

girl   2 sons   at least
                  3 more

Liu (grain merchant,
St. of Stone Bridge)

Yang ≠Nung En = Pomegranate Flower
(whore) (scholar) (14 at betrothal)
                   ("cold fish")

= second wife

boy
(aged 10 near
end of story)

at least
2 more

total Wang's grandchildren
11 boys & 8 girls

NOTES

NOTES

NOTES

NOTES